Contents

MW00902843

How to Use This Book

Language Development: Variety of Texts is intended to help learners develop their reading comprehension skills. The activities stimulate learners' interests by dealing with subject matter that is age appropriate. Both fiction and nonfiction content follows The National Council of Teachers of English (NCTE) standards for a wide range of fictional and nonfictional texts that deal with diverse subject matter and reading comprehension skills, making the activities suitable for school curriculum. The reading material is based on social studies and scientific subjects. The contents of this book allow learners to understand that information can come from a variety of sources. The activities incorporate the reading skills that learners already possess to enhance understanding of texts.

Language Development: Variety of Texts is divided into six sections: Fiction, Nonfiction, Storytelling, Reading for Information, Following Directions, and Write Your Own. Each section focuses on a specific standard for learning and applying reading comprehension and writing skills. The simple directions along with skill definitions make each activity an enjoyable learning process.

✏️ Fiction

This section focuses on various aspects of fictional material. Learners are challenged by activities about legends, folklore, and storytelling. As learners analyze the texts, they will gain an understanding of the differences between simple storytelling and larger-than-life legends and folklore.

✏️ Nonfiction

The nonfiction texts in this section allow learners to understand that informational text can help in learning about our world as well as history. The stories presented deal with historical figures in American history and information about animals in our natural world. The activities are designed to help learners focus and reflect on essential facts while reading.

✏️ Storytelling

Understanding how stories are told builds reading comprehension skills. This section stresses the first-person and the third-person points of view in storytelling. Each story allows learners to see how using a certain point of view in writing can help the presentation of the story. Working with these activities will allow learners to grasp storytelling skills that can be applied to their own writing.

✏️ Reading for Information

The activities in this section draw learners' attention to sources of information that are available. The sources are newspapers, magazines, the Internet, and encyclopedias. The activities develop a learner's ability to find and understand information from different types of media. Also, the activities show that each source is useful for certain types of factual information. For example, newspapers present news, while encyclopedias give facts about many aspects of our world.

✏️ Following Directions

Being able to follow directions is an important skill for learners. As learners examine the activities in this section, they will practice working with text that provides directional information. The activities use analytical skills to build reading comprehension.

✏️ Write Your Own

The activities in this section call for learners to write in four different forms: diary, story, directions, and a new ending. Each activity challenges learners to create text, building on their own storytelling abilities and motivating them to apply their imaginative thinking. These activities are designed to guide learners through the writing process in order to effectively communicate their ideas.

© Rosen School Supply•Brain Builders Variety of Texts•3•RSS

Name _____

Story Time

Fiction stories are stories that have been made up by a writer. The writer of the following story has created a story about a character who is writing a letter to his grandmother.

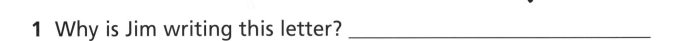 **Directions: Read this fictional letter, then answer the questions.**

Dear Grandma,

Today in school we learned all about cotton. Did you know cotton comes from a plant? Small seed pods on the cotton plant contain the seed. The seed has hair or fibers. As the seed pods get older, the amount of seed fibers grows. When they get older, the seed pods are picked and then the fibers are removed. The cotton is sent off to factories to be spun into cloth. Next week my teacher is taking us to a cotton farm. I'm very excited.

Love, Jim

1 Why is Jim writing this letter? _____

_____

2 What do seed pods contain? _____

3 Was Jim happy to learn about cotton? _____

4 Is this story real? _____

4

Name _____

Our World

Nonfiction stories give information about real events, places, and people.

> **Directions: Read the following nonfiction story to find out information about ocelots. Answer the questions by circling the correct answer.**

Ocelots are large spotted cats that live in the wild. They live in areas from Texas to Argentina. Ocelots can climb very well. They hunt for food at night. They eat fish, birds, lizards, and snakes. There are not very many ocelots left in the world. They have been hunted for their fur. Many places have laws to protect ocelots.

1 Ocelots live in
   A Asia
   B France
   C Argentina
   D New York City

2 Ocelots hunt for food
   A at sunrise
   B at noon
   C in the afternoon
   D at night

3 Ocelots eat
   A fish
   B lizards
   C snakes
   D all of the above

5

Name _____

First Person

Storytelling can be done in two ways. One way is done in the first person. In first-person storytelling, the person telling the story is part of the story.

Directions: Read the following story, then decide if the statements are true or false. Circle the correct answer.

My name is Jane. I am a Red Cross worker. The Red Cross helps people who have been affected by floods, earthquakes, and other problems. In my last assignment, my coworkers and I helped people whose homes had been flooded due to rainstorms. We made sure that those people had a safe place to stay and food to eat. We also made sure that anyone who needed medical attention got help.

1 Jane's job is to help people.
True   False

2 This story is told in the first person.
True   False

3 Jane works as a teacher for the Red Cross.
True   False

Name _____

Encyclopedia

When you read for information, you are trying to find out facts about a subject. Newspapers, encyclopedias, and magazines are some sources that provide information.

Directions: The following is an encyclopedia article about Juneteenth. See if you can find out all the facts about this holiday. Complete the sentences that follow.

Juneteenth is an American holiday that celebrates the end of slavery. It takes place on June 19th. On June 19th, 1865, the news reached Texas that slavery had been ended in the United States. This was two years after President Abraham Lincoln had issued the Emancipation Proclamation. The Emancipation Proclamation stated that all slaves in the United States were free.

1 Juneteenth celebrates the end of _____.

2 _____ signed the

Emancipation Proclamation in _____.

3 Juneteenth is celebrated on _____.

Name _____

Recipe

Following directions is an important skill that allows you to work on projects.

✏️ **Directions: Read the recipe for pumpkin soup below and answer the questions about it.**

Ingredients
8 oz. can of cooked pumpkin
1 cup of milk
1 teaspoon of olive oil
1 teaspoon sugar
1/4 teaspoon cinnamon
1/8 teaspoon nutmeg

Stir the pumpkin and the milk in a pot. The stove should be on low heat. Add the olive oil, the sugar, the cinnamon, and the nutmeg. Stir ingredients until everything is mixed.

1 What is the main ingredient of this recipe? _____

2 List the ingredients in the order they should be put into

the pot. _____

3 What kind of heat should the stove be on? _____

Name _____

Your Story

Creating your own story allows you to practice your writing and storytelling.

> **Directions: Write a story about a trip you took. Include the following details:**

1 Where did you go? What did you do?

2 What was the weather like? Did it affect your trip?

3 Who went along with you on your trip?

4 How long was your trip?

5 What was the most interesting thing about your trip?

_____

_____

_____

_____

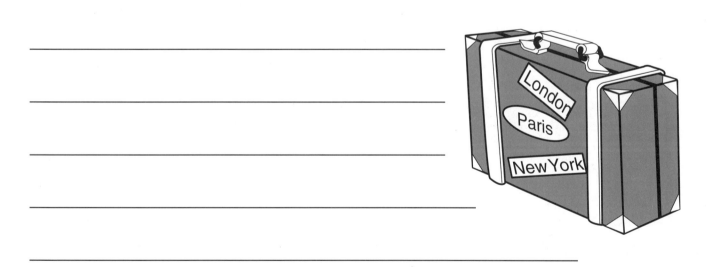

_____

_____

_____

Background

• The stories in this section help learners interpret different elements involved in reading fiction. Legends, folklore, or simple storytelling consist of a variety of elements that challenge learners into differentiating fiction from nonfiction. The activities provide a way to enhance reading skills.

Homework Helper

• Many stories about Paul Bunyan (p. 13) have circulated in American history. Have the learner use sources such as the Internet and the library to find out other Paul Bunyan stories.

Research-based Activity

• Working together with the learner, find out the history of the Paul Bunyan folklore. Identify how, where, and why it began.

Test Prep

• Fiction comprehension is part of state standards throughout the country. The reading comprehension skills that are part of the activities of this section are important for preparing learners for testing procedures.

Different Audiences

• To challenge accelerated learners, have them create fiction stories of their own. Letter writing, such as the form of the story on page 12, is an effective tool that learners can use to get their stories across to an audience.

Name _____

Pecos Bill and the Tornado

Folklore is a story that has been made up and passed down through time.

✏️➡ **Directions: Read the following story, then answer the questions about it.**

Pecos Bill was a cowboy who could ride any animal in the West. One day Pecos Bill even rode a tornado! The day the biggest tornado ever came to Kansas, Pecos Bill was ready for it. He jumped on and grabbed the tornado. The tornado flattened forests and twisted rivers trying to get rid of Pecos Bill. It bucked and jumped with all its might, but it could not throw Pecos Bill. Finally, it gave up and turned into rain, letting Pecos Bill fall to the ground.

1 Is this story fiction? _____

2 What job did Pecos Bill do? _____

3 What state did the tornado come to? _____

4 How did the tornado finally get rid of Pecos Bill? _____

_____

Name _____

Garter Snakes

Some fictional stories can contain facts even though the story itself is made up.

Directions: Read the following fictional letter, then answer the questions about it.

Dear Mom and Dad,

Summer camp is great. Today we went on a hike through the woods. We saw a garter snake by a stream. It had yellow stripes. Our guide told us that garter snakes are some of the most common snakes found in North America. She also told us that they eat fish, frogs, and even mice. Baby garter snakes eat worms and leeches. On our way back to camp, we collected leaves of many different trees.

See you soon, Eric

1 How does the person writing the letter feel about summer camp? _____

_____

2 What is the main subject of the story? _____

Challenge: Write a story about your favorite animal. Read it out loud to your parents.

Name _____

Paul Bunyan

Legends are stories that have been around for a long time.

✏️ **Directions: Read the following legend, then answer the questions about it.**

Paul Bunyan was a giant. When Paul was a baby, he was too big to sleep in his parents' home. His father put Paul's cradle in a large ship so that the waves could rock the baby to sleep. When Paul grew up, he was so big that he used a pine tree to comb his beard. Paul worked as a logger. A logger's job is cutting down trees. Loggers have to be very strong. One day, Paul was walking by a great river when he heard a woman yelling for help. Paul quickly blocked up the river with mountains and trees and saved the woman.

1 The theme of this story is Paul Bunyan's
   A beard **B** size
   C cradle **D** parents

2 How do you know that this story is fiction?

_____

3 What kind of work does Paul Bunyan do?

_____

Challenge: Using the Internet, find out what kinds of tools loggers use in their work.

13

Name _____

Molly Pitcher

Legends are stories that have been around for a long time, though no one is sure if they really happened. Some legends are based on real events and people.

Directions: Read the following legend, then answer the questions about it.

My name is Mary Ludwig. I lived during colonial times. I'm also known as Molly Pitcher. I got my nickname during the American Revolutionary War. During a battle in New Jersey, the American soldiers camped out near my home. One hot day during the battle, I decided to take water to the soldiers. Taking a large pitcher, I rode my horse to the battlefield. I saw that the men were tired and very thirsty. I filled my pitcher at a nearby spring and took the water to the soldiers. Some men who knew me called out, "Molly, pitcher!" Other men, thinking that this was my name, also called, "Here, Molly Pitcher!"

1 What did Molly take with her to the battlefield? _____

_____

2 How does Molly get her nickname? _____

_____

3 What war were the soldiers fighting? _____

_____

14

Name _____

Skill Check—Fiction

✏️ **Directions: Read the following fictional stories, then answer the questions about them.**

Legend

John Henry worked on the American railroad that was built in the 1870s. John was known for his great strength. He drove spikes into solid rock. One day, his boss brought a machine that would replace workers like John Henry. John was very upset about this. He decided to race the machine to see if he could drive spikes faster than it. At the end of the race, John Henry was the winner.

1 Who is the main character in this story? _____

2 When does the story take place? _____

3 What kind of work did John Henry do? _____

Story Time

Sally and her parents went to visit Washington, D.C., which is the capital of the United States. Sally saw many exciting places in Washington, D.C. Sally and her parents visited the Smithsonian Institution, a museum. They also visited Capitol Hill, Sally's favorite place.

1 Who are the characters in the story? _____

2 What places did Sally visit? _____

3 This story is fiction. **True**   **False**

Background

• The nonfiction text in this section focuses on giving information about our world as well as information about important people in our country's history. These curriculum-based stories allow learners to connect with their world.

Homework Helper

• Ask the learner to create a nonfiction story about his or her favorite animal. Have the learner describe the animal's physical traits: height, weight, and any distinguishing features, such as an elephant's trunk or a rhinoceros's horns. The story must consist of facts about the animal's food, habitat, offspring, and life span.

Research-based Activity

• Using an encyclopedia, work with the learner to find out where the coral reefs around the world are located. Then use an atlas to find the various locations.

Test Prep

• Activities such as the matching activity on page 19 allow the learner to approach the text as well as testing questions in a creative manner.

Different Audiences

• For English-as-a-Second-Language learners, have them translate "Giraffes" on page 17. This will help them grasp the concepts in the English version.

Name _____

Giraffes

We read nonfiction writing to find out more about our world and its living things.

> **Directions: Read the following story, then circle the correct answer to the questions.**

Giraffes are the tallest land animals in the world. Most giraffes grow to be 16 to 18 feet tall. A giraffe's long neck has the same number of bones as a human's neck does. Giraffes eat twigs and leaves from the highest branches of trees. The acacia (ah-KAY-shuh) tree is a favorite of giraffes. Acacias grow on the grasslands in Africa, where many giraffes live.

1 Giraffes live in _____.
   A Asia   **B** Africa
   C South America   **D** North America

2 The tallest animals in the world are _____.
   A gorillas   **B** snakes
   C whales   **D** giraffes

3 Giraffes like to eat twigs and leaves from _____.
   A the maple tree   **B** the oak tree
   C the acacia tree   **D** the apple tree

4 A giraffe's neck has the same number of bones as a human _____.
   A hand   **B** neck
   C leg   **D** arm

Challenge: Name another animal that lives in Africa. Write five sentences describing that animal.

17

Name _____

Annie Oakley

Nonfiction stories can tell us information about history.

✏️ **Directions: Read the story about Annie Oakley. Answer the questions about the story.**

Annie Oakley was one of the best sharpshooters of the late 1800s. She became the main attraction in Buffalo Bill's Wild West show. Annie could hit a target behind her by using a mirror. She could shatter glass balls tossed into the air. Annie was such an expert sharpshooter that she even impressed Sitting Bull, the Sioux chief. Sitting Bull called her Little Sure Shot. When Thomas Edison invented the movie camera, he had Annie do her act for some of the first movies that he made.

1 What is this story about?
   A Annie Oakley's horse   **B** Buffalo Bill's Wild West show
   C Annie Oakley's   **D** Thomas Edison's
   sharpshooting ability   movie camera

2 Why did Sitting Bull call Annie Oakley Little Sure Shot?

_____

3 List one thing that Annie Oakley would
   shoot during Buffalo Bill's Wild West show. _____

Challenge: Name five things that a cowboy would have used or worn. Draw pictures showing a cowboy using or wearing these things.

Name _____

Polyps

We read nonfiction writing to find out more about our world and its living things.

> ✏️ **Directions: Read the following story, then match the word in Column One to the correct description in Column Two.**

Coral is an underwater community made up of sea creatures called polyps. Polyps come in different colors and sizes. They look like branches of trees or tiny pipes and tubes. Coral is formed in the ocean when polyps die. Millions of polyp skeletons turn into a hard rock called limestone. Coral gets bigger when new, live polyps attach themselves to the limestone. Polyps cannot swim. They count on the moving ocean water to carry food to them. There are many plants and sea creatures living near the coral that polyps can eat.

Column One	Column Two
1 Polyps	A carries food
2 Limestone	B polyps
3 Food	C underwater community
4 Ocean	D hard rock
5 Sea creatures	E plants and sea creatures
6 Coral	F different colors and sizes

Name _____

John Muir

Nonfiction stories can tell us information about history.

✏️ **Directions: Read the following story, then answer the questions about it.**

John Muir traveled around the world studying natural areas. He wrote about what he saw in magazine articles and books. He worked hard to make people aware of the environment. Before Yosemite National Park in California became a protected area, too many of its trees were being cut down. John got people interested in Yosemite. In 1890, Congress made Yosemite a national park. John helped to protect many other wild places. Today, John is called the father of the national parks because of his work.

1 The passage tells of John Muir's work to make people aware of the environment. **True   False**

2 Why is John Muir called the father of the national parks?

_____

3 What is the name of the area that Congress turned into a

national park? _____

Name _____

Skill Check—Nonfiction

➤ **Directions: Read the following stories, then answer the questions about them.**

History

George Washington Carver found hundreds of ways to use peanuts, sweet potatoes, and soybeans. This led farmers in the South to start growing crops other than cotton. He discovered a way to get dyes of red, purple, and blue from clay.

1 George Washington Carver worked as a farmer. **True   False**

2 How did Carver's discoveries help farmers in the South?

_____

Our World

Box turtles live in the eastern and central parts of the United States. They eat worms, insects, berries, and leaves. Box turtles make their homes on dry land. Though most box turtles live for about 40 years, some have lived for about one hundred years.

1 Where do box turtles live? _____

2 How long do box turtles live? _____

3 What do box turtles eat? _____

Teaching Tips...

Background

• In this section, the stories are told in either the first person or the third person. In first-person storytelling, the narrator is a part of the story. He or she tells the story using "I" to refer to him or herself. In third-person storytelling, the narrator is outside of the story. The details of the story are stated.

Homework Helper

• Have the learner write two paragraphs about a holiday. In the first paragraph, the learner will use the first-person form of storytelling to describe his or her experience on that holiday. In the second paragraph, the learner will use the third-person form of storytelling to give the history of the holiday.

Research-based Activity

• Working together with the learner, use the library to find video documentaries to learn more about the history of the Nile.

Test Prep

• The learner understands writing conventions and will be able to apply these methods of narration to understand text. The learner will also be able to apply these conventions to his or her own writing.

Different Audiences

• When working with an accelerated learner, have the learner find various reading sources that have both first-person and third-person narration.

The Nile River

In first-person storytelling, the person telling the story is part of the story.

✏️ **Directions: Read the following story, then answer the questions about it.**

My name is Abdul. The year is 2927 B.C. I live in Egypt near the banks of the Nile River. In the summertime, the river rises so high that it floods the land. The floods leave thick black mud that helps my father's crops grow. However, sometimes the flooding gets out of control. Our homes, which are made of mud bricks, fall apart during the floods. Until 2925 B.C., Egypt was divided into two lands called Upper and Lower Egypt. The people of these separate lands fought each other for power. Then they realized that life would be easier if they worked together to control the floods. King Menes is our ruler now.

1 What is the storyteller's name? _____

2 Why did the people from Upper and Lower Egypt fight

each other? _____

3 Why did the people join together? _____

4 Who ruled Egypt in 2927 B.C.? _____

Challenge: Place yourself in another time. Write four sentences about yourself living in that time. Use the library to find out more information about the period.

Name _____

Third Person

The Trojan Horse

In third-person storytelling, the storyteller is not in the story. The events of the story are given to the reader.

Directions: Read the following story. Solve the crossword puzzle by answering the questions about the story.

When Prince Paris of Troy stole Queen Helen of Greece, a war started. It lasted for 10 years outside of Troy. The Greek soldiers decided to trick the Trojans. They built a large wooden horse and hid inside of it. The Trojans found the horse and took it into their city. They thought the Greeks had left and began to celebrate the end of the war. When the Trojans were asleep, the Greeks climbed out of the horse and rescued Queen Helen.

Across
1 Whom did the Greeks try to rescue?
2 Who stole Helen?
4 How many years did the war last?
5 The Trojans began to do this when they thought the Greeks left.
6 What was the horse made of?

Down
1 What did the Greeks build?
3 Who tricked the Trojans?
4 Where was the war fought?

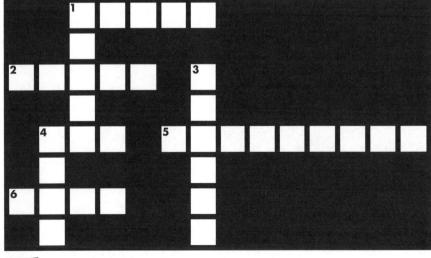

Name _____

My Day at the Zoo

In first-person storytelling, the person telling the story is part of the story.

Directions: Read the following story, then circle the correct answers to the questions.

I'm at Insect World. It is the part of the zoo where the bugs live. Most bugs are called insects. Here at Insect World there are bugs everywhere! My favorite part is the Butterfly House. The butterflies fly around as visitors walk through the Butterfly House. I look through a special camera that shows a close-up view of leaf-cutter ants. They cut pieces of leaves and take them underground to make food. I can't wait to see the rest of the exhibit.

1 This story is told in the
   A First person   **B** Third person

2 Circle the answer that is **not** true.
   The person telling the story:
   A Likes insects
   B Is sad to be at the zoo
   C Is excited to be at the zoo
   D Likes the butterfly display

3 Insect World is the part of the zoo where people can learn more about insects.
   True   False

Name _____

Carlsbad Caverns

In third-person storytelling, the storyteller is not in the story. The events of the story are given to the reader.

> **Directions: Read the following story, then circle the correct answers to the questions.**

Mrs. James's third grade class is on a field trip at the Carlsbad Caverns. The Carlsbad Caverns are a series of underground caverns in New Mexico. The students are excited as they enter the caverns. Their guide tells them that the caverns were discovered by a cowboy named Jim White. They learn that the caverns were one solid limestone rock at the bottom of an ocean 250 million years ago. Over the years, water that got into cracks in the rock ate away at it. The result is the spectacular caverns. In the various caves, the class finds shapes called speleothems. These shapes look like icicles, curtains, spikes, and frozen rivers.

1 Who discovered the Carlsbad Caverns?
   A Mrs. James **B** Jim White
   C The guide   **D** None of the above

2 The icicles, curtains, spikes, and frozen rivers are shapes called
   A speleothems **B** caverns
   C limestone   **D** None of the above

3 Two hundred and fifty million years ago, the Carlsbad Caverns were one solid limestone rock.   **True   False**

26

Name _____

Skill Check—Storytelling
Third Person

> **Directions: Read the following story, then circle the correct answer to each question.**

The Moon

Earth's moon is the brightest object in the night sky. The light from the Moon is light that is reflected from the Sun. Half of the Moon is always lit by the Sun. When people on Earth see a full moon, the lit side of the Moon is facing Earth. When only half of the Moon is seen, only half of the lit side of the Moon is facing Earth.

1 The brightest object in the night sky is
   A Mars   **B** the Moon   **C** the Sun

2 The Moon's light comes from
   A Jupiter   **B** Earth   **C** the Sun

3 A full moon means
   A The side of the Moon that is lit is facing Earth
   B Half of the lit side of the Moon is facing Earth
   C The Sun is in the sky

Teaching Tips...

TEACHING TIPS

Background

• Reading for information is important for conducting research and understanding issues about the world. Newspapers, magazines, encyclopedias, and the Internet are some sources for information. Newspapers provide information about the world. Your town newspapers provide news about the weather and local events. From nature to politics, magazines are resources for information on many things in our world. Encyclopedias are important research tools. We can find out many important facts about the world we live in. Educational and news Web sites on the Internet can be great sources for finding information.

Homework Helper

• Learners should practice research methods. Have the learner find out more about hurricanes by using different research sources. The learner should then compare the findings from the various sources to see how they differ.

Research-based Activity

• Ask the learner to use the newspaper to find articles about places around the world. Ask the learner to answer the following questions: Why was the article written? Where is the place located? Who are the people in the article?

Test Prep

• Research becomes more important as learners progress in their writing. By learning to use the proper resources for research, learners will be meeting state standards.

Different Audiences

• To challenge learners, have them pick out subjects that are interesting to them. Have the learners research those subjects in encyclopedias and magazines. Discuss the information that was found and how this information differed from information that the learners may have already known about the subjects.

Name _____

Blizzard

We read news stories for daily information about our community. News stories must answer the five questions: who, what, why, where, and when. These questions are known as the five Ws.

✏️➤ **Directions: Read the following news story, then find the five Ws.**

February 17, 2004

Last night in Chicago, Illinois, there was a blizzard that left snow two and a half feet deep. People are busy digging their way out of their homes. They are also digging out their cars. The snow is continuing to fall heavily. People are being warned to stay indoors. Businesses and schools are closed for the day.

Can you pick out the five **W**s in the news story?

Whom is this story about? _____

What is happening? _____

Why is the story important? _____

Where is the story taking place? _____

When is the story taking place? _____

Challenge: Create your own news story about an interesting event that happened in your life. Share your story with your parents or a friend.

29

Name _____

Orb Weaver

Nature magazines provide stories about animals and our world.

Directions: Read the following, then answer questions about it.

Orb weavers are spiders. They live in every part of the world except Antarctica. They are known for their wheel-shaped webs called orb webs. Orb weavers come in many different sizes. Tiny orb weavers make webs small enough to fit between two blades of grass. Large orb weavers can make orb webs that reach across wide streams.

　　Orb weavers use different kinds of silk to make webs. Orb weavers use dry silk for the edges of the web and sticky silk around the middle. The spiders wait for insects to fly into their sticky webs. Orb webs can be found in gardens and grass, around trees, or in dark corners.

1 What is the topic of this article? _____

2 Orb weavers can be found in every part of the world.
True　False

3 You may find an orb weaver's web in your backyard.
True　False

4 Give three details about an orb weaver's web. _____

_____

Challenge: Name another type of spider that lives in
　　　　　　North America.

Name _____

Hurricanes

Encyclopedias provide information on many things in our world.

> ✏️ **Directions: Read the following encyclopedia article. Then answer the questions about the article.**

Hurricanes are storms that start in the warm, tropical air of the southern Atlantic and the eastern Pacific Oceans. Storms gather heat and moisture from the warm ocean water. Winds near the oceans' surfaces form thunderstorms. Clouds rise high into the sky, taking moisture with them. When the winds reach 74 miles per hour, a storm becomes a full-grown hurricane. When a hurricane is over warm water, it can be active for more than two weeks.

1 Hurricanes are types of
   A rain   **B** storms   **C** winds   **D** droughts

2 Storms gather _____ and _____ to grow into hurricanes.

3 Winds in a hurricane reach at least _____ miles per hour.

Name _____

Gems

The Internet can be a great source of information about our world.

Directions: Read the following information from a Web site, then answer the questions about gems.

A mineral is solid matter that comes from the earth. There are more than 2,000 minerals. However, only 100 of these are called gems. Most gems are made from minerals that are found in many different kinds of rocks. Heat and pressure deep inside Earth can change the minerals in rocks into beautiful crystals. Gems also are made by animals and plants. Pearls are made inside clams, oysters, and mussels. Amber is what is left of the sap of very old pine trees. Most gems that are found look dull. These gems are polished and shaped to make them sparkle.

1 Why are gems polished and shaped? _____

2 Where are pearls made? _____

3 What two things cause minerals in rocks to turn into gems?

_____

Name _____

Skill Check—Reading for Information

✏️➡️ **Directions: Read the following stories, then answer the questions about them.**

News Story

Mayor Smith of Spring Town was at the opening of Trolley Park yesterday, May 13. Many of Spring Town's residents showed up to see the park. The park has a basketball court and two tennis courts. There is a playground with swings and slides. The mayor encouraged everyone to come out and enjoy the new park.

1 What is this story about? _____

2 Where is the park located? _____

3 Who are the people in the story? _____

Magazine Article

Ellen Ochoa is the first female Hispanic astronaut. Ochoa is also an inventor. She has three patents for her inventions. A patent is an official document that gives an inventor the right to make and sell his or her product.

1 Ellen Ochoa is an _____

and an _____.

2 What is a patent? _____

_____.

Teaching Tips...

TEACHING TIPS

Background

• Often learning is directly related to reading for directions. Reading for directions is an important skill that allows the learner to apply what is read directly to a project.

Homework Helper

• Using the Clocks activity on page 37 as an example, have the learner draw four diagrams showing 9 o'clock, 9:15, 9:30, and 9:45.

Research-based Activity

• Cooking from recipes is a fun way for learners to understand the concept of following directions. Work together with the learner to create a recipe of his or her choice. Use the Internet to get ideas for simple cooking.

Test Prep

• The activities in this section reflect the state standard requirement of reading a variety of texts.

Different Audiences

• ESL learners should practice reading directions in English as much as possible. When working with an ESL learner, have him or her translate the directions for the exercises in this section into his or her own language. This will help the learner grasp the language concepts that are in English.

Name _____

Mindy's Bus Ride

Schedules are ways to organize information about time.

▭▶ **Directions: Read the following story, then answer the questions by looking at the bus schedule.**

Mindy is taking the bus to the library, which is on Pine Drive. However, she is not sure what time the bus will be at her stop. Mindy has to check the bus schedule. She has to get on the bus at 12th Street. The street names are at the beginning of each row. The times the bus will be at the stop on each street are shown in that row.

Name of Stop	First Trip	Second Trip	Third Trip
Walnut Drive	8:00 A.M.	11:00 A.M.	2:00 P.M.
12th Street	9:00 A.M.	12:00 P.M.	3:00 P.M.
Prospect Street	9:15 A.M.	12:15 P.M.	3:15 P.M.
Oak Lane	9:30 A.M.	12:30 P.M.	3:30 P.M.
Pine Drive	10:00 A.M.	1:00 P.M.	4:00 P.M.

1 What times will the bus stop at 12th Street? _____

2 If Mindy gets on the bus at 9:00 A.M.,
   what time will she get to Pine Drive? _____

3 How long does the bus take to
   travel from 12th Street to Pine Drive? _____

Challenge: Create a schedule for your school day. Include the names of your classes and the times. Don't forget to add the time you take lunch.

35

Name _____

Cookies

Being able to follow directions is an important skill that allows you to work on projects.

✏️➤ **Directions: Put the second part of the recipe directions in the order they should be followed.**

Ingredients
1 egg
1 cup of butter
3 cups of flour
1 1/2 cups of powdered sugar
1 teaspoon of vanilla
1/4 teaspoon of baking powder

First, preheat oven to 375 degrees. Next, in a large bowl, stir the powdered sugar and butter together until they turn to a creamy mixture. Add the egg and vanilla and stir some more. Finally, add the flour and baking powder to make dough. Cover the dough and let it sit for two hours.

The following is the second part of the directions. Put these directions in order by numbering them 1 through 4.

_____ Place the shapes on a cookie sheet and bake for 10 minutes.

_____ Cut your favorite shapes out of the dough.

_____ Let the cookies cool before eating.

_____ After two hours, roll the dough out on a floured surface.

36

Name _____

How to Tell Time

Being able to read and follow directions can help you learn new skills.

✏️ **Directions: Read the directions for telling time, then answer the questions.**

The numbers on the face of a clock show hours and minutes. The hours are the large numbers 1 through 12. The minutes are represented by the small markings between the numbers.

minute hand

The hands on the clock show the time. The large hand is called the hour hand. It points to the numbers and tells us the hour. The small hand is called the minute hand. It points to the markings between the numbers and tells us the minute. When the minute hand points to 12, the time is exactly the hour that the hour hand is pointing to.

hour hand

6 o'clock

On this clock, the hour hand is pointing to one and the minute hand is pointing to 12. The time is 1:12.

1 A What time does this clock tell us? _____

B Explain how you know this. _____

_____

2 A The hour hand is pointing to _____

37

Name _____

Sprouting Beans

Being able to follow directions is an important skill that allows you to work on projects.

➡ **Directions: Read the following directions, then answer the questions.**

Have you ever wondered how plants grow? Try this experiment and see for yourself. Gather together an empty jar, cheesecloth, and a rubber band. You'll need two dozen dried garbanzo beans.

Put the beans in a jar and fill the jar halfway with water. Let the beans soak overnight. In the morning, drain all of the water and rinse the beans thoroughly. Cover the jar with the cheesecloth. Use the rubber band to hold it in place. Next, turn the jar upside down to completely drain all of the water. Place the jar with the beans in a warm spot out of the sun.

For the next three days, rinse the beans every morning and evening. Remember to drain completely. In just two to four days, you will have sprouts that you can even eat!

1 List the four items that you will need to start this project.

_____   _____

_____   _____

2 How long should the beans soak? _____

3 It is important to drain the beans completely after each rinse.
True   False

Name _____

Skill Check—Following Directions

Instructions

> ✏️➡ **Directions: Read the following directions, then answer the questions.**

Make six holes in the ground with a pencil. The holes should be about 1 inch deep and about one and a half feet apart. Place one sunflower seed in each hole. Mark each hole with a straw. Cover each hole with earth. Water your sunflowers daily. When they get tall enough, tie your sunflowers to stakes so that they don't fall over.

1 How often should the sunflowers get water? _____

_____

2 Why should you mark the holes with straws? _____

_____

3 How deep should you plant the sunflower seeds? _____

_____

4 Why should you tie the sunflowers to the stakes? _____

_____

5 How far apart should you plant the seeds? _____

_____

Background

• By practicing writing, learners will discover how to communicate their thoughts and ideas effectively. These exercises allow learners to write by applying many of the writing methods discovered from reading.

Homework Helper

• Have the learner keep a journal. In the journal, the learner should keep a record of daily or weekly events that affect him or her. This practice will help the learner express his or her thoughts and ideas.

Research-based Activity

• Using an encyclopedia or the Internet, work with the learner to find information about his or her favorite writer. Use the information to create a story about the writer's life.

Test Prep

• As prescribed in state standards, learners need to understand how to use writing for their own purposes.

Different Audiences

• Have the learner choose his or her favorite short story, then rewrite the ending. He or she should think about the elements of the story's ending that he or she likes or dislikes. The learner should consider the events in the story that affect the ending and how those events should be altered.

Name _____

The Circus

Diaries are logs people keep of their lives. Some people may write in them as often as every day. Others may write only once a month.

Directions: On a separate sheet of paper, write about something interesting that happened to you recently. Include the following details: date, place, the names of the people who were involved, and how you felt about the event.

Example:

Dear Diary,   August 12

Today I went to the circus with my parents. We saw many performers. My favorites were the clowns and acrobats. I thought the clowns were very funny. The little boy sitting next to us didn't think so. He thought they were scary. The acrobats performed amazing tricks. They even did some stunts on wires high above the ring. That was scary!

Challenge: Make two columns. In the first column, give the names of three caverns. In the second column, give their locations.

41

Name _____

Let's Play

Creating your own story helps you practice writing.

> **Directions:** Pick a game you like to play. Write directions for playing this game. Include the following details.

1 What is the name of the game?
2 How many players does the game require?
3 What kind of equipment does the game need?
4 Is a score kept? If so, how?

_____

_____

_____

_____

_____

_____

_____

_____

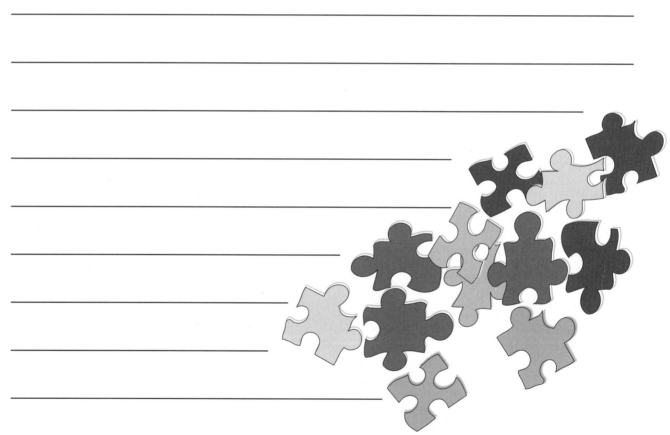

Challenge: Work with a friend. Each of you pick your favorite sport. List the things about your sport that you like and read them to each other.

42

Name _____

Daedalus and Icarus

In predicting the outcome of a story, you create your own ending of the story.

Directions: Read the following story, then write your own ending to the story.

King Minos of Greece had put Icarus and his father, Daedalus, in prison. The prison was surrounded by the sea with no way to escape. Daedalus came up with a plan to escape. He made two sets of wings—one for Icarus and one for himself. Before they flew away, Daedalus warned Icarus not to fly too close to the sun. The sun could melt the glue on the wings. Icarus, however, was excited at being able to fly. He kept flying higher and higher.

What do you think happened to Icarus?

_____

_____

_____

_____

_____

Challenge: Find out the real ending to this story through your library or the Internet. Compare it to your ending.

Name _____

Your Story

Creating your own story allows you to practice writing.

> **Directions:** On a separate piece of paper, write a story based on a day spent in a park. Tell the story as if it were happening to you. Take two of your friends along. Include the following details:

1 What day is it?

2 What is the weather like?

3 Do you and your friends play a game at the park?

4 Do you need equipment such as a tennis racket or a basketball to play the game?

5 Is there a playground at the park? Do you play on the swings or the jungle gym?

6 Do you meet any people you know at the park?

Challenge: Is there a famous park in your state? Find out its history. How did it become a park?

Name _____

Skill Check—Write Your Own

Story

> Directions: On a separate sheet of paper, write a letter to your friend about your summer vacation.

Include activities that you did, how you felt about the activities, people you may have met, comments on the weather, and places you visited. Was there one really interesting thing that you did? Don't forget to sign your letter.

Predictions

> Directions: Read the following story, then write your own ending to the story. Write your story on a separate sheet of paper.

Jan is a runner on her school's track and field team. The first race of the year is tomorrow. Today, she is practicing with the team. As the team warms up, the coach tells them that there may be rain tomorrow. Everyone is disappointed to hear that. They have worked very hard to get ready for the race.

45

Answer Key

p. 4
1) Jim is writing to tell his grandmother about what he learned in school.
2) seeds
3) Yes
4) No, it is fiction.

p. 5
1) C
2) D
3) D

p. 6
1) True
2) True
3) False

p. 7
1) slavery
2) President Abraham Lincoln, 1863
3) June 19th

p. 8
1) pumpkin
2) pumpkin, milk, olive oil, sugar, cinnamon, and nutmeg
3) low heat

p. 11
1) Yes
2) cowboy
3) Kansas
4) The tornado turned into rain.

p. 12
1) He likes summer camp.
2) garter snakes

p. 13
1) B
2) There are more than three possible answers to this question. They include: Paul Bunyan was giant. His cradle was a large ship. He combed his beard with a pine tree. He blocked up the river with mountains and trees.
3) He was a logger.

p. 14
1) a pitcher
2) by the soldiers calling for her to bring them water
3) the American Revolutionary War

p. 15
Legend
1) John Henry
2) 1870s
3) He worked on the railroad, driving spikes into solid rock.

Story Time
1) Sally and her parents
2) The Smithsonian Institution and Capitol Hill
3) True

p. 17
1) B
2) D
3) C
4) B

p. 18
1) C
2) Annie Oakley impressed Sitting Bull with her shooting ability.
3) glass balls thrown in the air

p. 19
1) F
2) D
3) E
4) A
5) B
6) C

p. 20
1) True
2) John Muir was called the father of the national parks because of his work to protect wild places.
3) Yosemite National Park

p. 21
History
1) False
2) Farmers in the South started growing crops other than cotton.

Our World
1) the eastern and central parts of the United States
2) Most box turtles live for 40 years. Some live for about a hundred years.
3) worms, insects, berries, and leaves

p. 23
1) Abdul
2) for power
3) They had to work together to control the floods.
4) King Menes

p. 24
Across
1) Helen
2) Paris
4) ten
5) celebrate
6) wood
Down
1) horse
3) Greeks
4) Troy

p. 25
1) A
2) B
3) True

p. 26
1) B
2) A
3) True

p. 27
Storytelling
1) B
2) C
3) A

p. 29
1) residents of Chicago
2) a blizzard
3) The story is being written to let people know how their daily lives are being affected by the blizzard.
4) Chicago
5) February 17, 2004

p. 30
1) orb weavers
2) False
3) True
4) wheel-shaped; made of silk; can be very small or very large; made of sticky silk in the middle; found in gardens and grass, around trees, or in dark corners

47

p. 31
1) B
2) heat and moisture
3) 74

p. 32
1) to make them sparkle
2) in clams, oysters and mussels
3) heat and pressure

p. 33
Newstory
1) the opening of Trolley Park
2) Spring Town
3) Mayor Smith and the town's residents

Magazine Article
1) Ellen Ochoa is an astronaut and an inventor.
2) A patent is an official document that gives an inventor the right to make and sell his or her product.

p. 35
1) 9:00 A.M., 12:00 P.M., 3:00 P.M.
2) 10:00 A.M.
3) One hour

p. 36
3
2
4
1

p. 37
1) **A** 3:00 **B** When the minute hand points to 12, the time is exactly the hour that the hour hand is pointing to.
2) **A** 8

p. 38
1) garbanzo beans, an empty jar, cheesecloth, and a rubber band
2) overnight
3) True

p. 39
Instructions
1) every day
2) so that you can tell where you planted the sunflowers
3) 1 inch deep
4) so that they don't fall over
5) about one and a half feet apart